5:2 Diet

Meal Plans & Recipes

by Liz Armond

Published in United Kingdom

© Copyright 2014 – Liz Armond

ISBN-13: 978-1511981040
ISBN-10: 1511981040

Table of Contents

Introduction

Losing weight can be difficult, and knowing which diet to try can be harder. The 5:2 Diet has quickly become one of the most popular diets around to help you lose and maintain weight loss.

5:2 Diet Meal Plans and Recipes will make it so much easier to stick to this diet because you now have recipes that will help you achieve your weight loss goals.

I have lost a significant amount of weight with this diet and wanted to find easy to prepare and cook food that didn't need expensive and hard to find ingredients.

Because I couldn't seem to find the recipes that suited my needs I researched and put together my own cookbook **Recipes for the 5:2 Diet** which was warmly received.

I think this was mainly because the recipes did not require tedious work or fancy ingredients. They are low calorie and healthy, but are put together with the basics available in your home.

These meal plans are adapted from the recipes in that cookbook and designed to make life simple for those with a busy schedule or don't have the inclination to plan out their weekly diet days.

I hope that you enjoy my recipes, and get to enjoy cooking and eating food that is also quick and easy to prepare.

I enjoy being creative with my food, and I urge you to do the same. For example, try adding a little more spice, extra vegetables, or a different stock.

Finally, many of the recipes in this cookbook can be adapted for those not dieting in your family. You simply add potatoes, rice, or pasta as liked.

Above all else, enjoy your food and the process of cooking it. You are only dieting for two days a week, so it is not necessary to stress. However, you will find that over time, you will start noticing labels and calories much more than you used to

About the 5:2 Fast Diet

The 5:2 Diet or Fast Diet or Intermittent Diet are just a few of the names given to a currently very popular way of losing weight, so called because generally speaking you can eat normally on 5 days a week but on the other 2 days, known as fasting days you must restrict your food and drink intake to only 500 calories if you are female or 600 calories if you are a male. This is regardless of your current weight or how much you need to lose.

Because this book is a collection of meal plans with recipes, I'm assuming that you are following the diet and that it is working for you. Perhaps you are tired of cooking the same recipes and are now looking for some different foods to eat. But for those of you who are new to the diet I will summarise the main points of the 5:2 Diet to give you a quick start guide.

It doesn't really matter which days you choose to feed or fast but it is generally recommended that the fasting days are not done together although it won't hurt every once in a while. Depending on the speed you wish to lose the weight you could also adjust the ratio of fasting to feeding days. For example you could try a 6:1 or 4:3 etc.

When you have reached your ideal weight perhaps then is the time to consider fasting for just one day a week to maintain your ideal weight, but for now let's assume you have a goal to reach, so we will a look at the normal 5:2 diet in more depth.

On fasting days you can elect to consume all of your calories in one go, or more what is more usual is to spread them throughout the day. Breakfast can either be a really low calorie count which means you can probably have a light lunch as well or you can skip it altogether.

I found skipping breakfast worked better for me as it didn't kick start my juices first thing and I had no problem lasting until midday lunch. I quite often forgot all about food and went to 1 or 2 o'clock before I realised I was getting hungry. I don't think I could eat breakfast and then have nothing until my evening meal unless I was seriously fasting, meaning I was going without all food for that day. I cover this in more depth in my book **Fasting Your Way to Health**

There is varying opinion on whether filling up at breakfast or snacking throughout the day is more effective for weight loss. You will find your own preferred method, I tried both and found that splitting my calories between lunch and dinner worked better for me but then I can manage to skip breakfast, you may not be able to.

Drink plenty of fluids including some tea or coffee as this will fill your empty stomach but no sugar, try agave natural sugar substitute if you have to have a sweetener and watch your milk intake or you will quickly eat into your calories. But please don't worry about going over the 500 calories by a bit because when you do follow this eating plan you will be amazed at how you start to look at everything you eat on your 'normal' days and will in fact eat less anyway.

You could try fizzy water or diet soda and some people have suggested chewing sugar free gum although I found that made me hungry.

On your five normal days you can eat whatever you like within reason. This is to say you should load your system with unhealthy fast or junk food. What you will find is that you are looking at packaging much more than you used to. You will be shocked at the amount of calories in one chocolate biscuit, I know I was. If you think about the calories in that one biscuit and then think of the percentage that biscuit is of your 500 or 600 calorie allowance on your fasting days you quickly come to appreciate why that weight crept on in the first place.

Remember if the hunger pangs become too much, do something active like going for a walk. You can drink as much water as you like and this will fill you up too. Try a little honey or lemon juice in a glass of warm water, you will soon feel full until your meal is due. If you are doing this with your partner, don't forget to factor in an additional 100 calories if you or your partner is male.

If you are worried about the long term effects on

your body, contrary to what some people think, fasting can be a healthy way to lose weight. It can reduce levels of IGF-1 (insulin-like growth factor 1, which can lead to accelerated ageing). It can also 'switch' on DNA repair genes as well as reducing blood pressure and lowering cholesterol and glucose levels.

A word of warning, it is not recommended for pregnant women or diabetics on medication. In fact anyone who has health problems or has an existing medical condition is strongly advised to consult their GP first. This is not to say you can't follow this diet, it is just so it can be done under medical advice or supervision.

Finally, keep going by thinking to yourself that this is only for 2 days a week, you are not on a full blown 7 days a week diet for weeks on end or in some cases what seems forever.

Finally, if you are interested in other methods of fasting, I do cover this in my book on losing weight through fasting called, 'Fasting Your Way to Health

Who Should NOT Fast?

The 5:2 fast will have very little adverse effect on many of the following groups, but use your common sense

1. Infants and children. There is really no good reason for infants and children to fast. Due to their lack of maturity, they would likely not really understand the spiritual purpose of fasting, and their growing bodies need to take in ample nutrients regularly.

2. Pregnant or nursing women. Most fasts, including the 5:2 should be avoided by women who are pregnant or nursing unless cleared by a Doctor. The baby requires so many nutrients for normal development and is dependent on the mother's proper nutrition to receive those nutrients. You are forcing the unborn baby to fast and can be potentially dangerous to both mother and child.

3. People with Cancer - Do not fast unless you are

fasting in an attempt to help yourself heal in which case this should be under direct medical advice. The 5:2 is probably not severe enough for this purpose. Cancer is usually indicative of, amongst other things, an immune system that is not in good shape.

4. People with other health concerns. The 5:2 Fast Diet is a good way to regulate food intake on overweight or obese sufferers and juice fasts may be another option. However check with your Doctor first as he may wish to supervise your weight loss.

5. The Elderly - There is no need for the elderly to fast as their body may not be able to manage such a task but it may not hurt them to lose a little weight for mobility reasons. Again use your common sense and perhaps only try 1 day intermittent fasting to start.

And if anyone still has any concerns or questions, they should always ask their doctor. Remember, fasting is supposed to help bring out the best of health for us.

Useful Cooking Guide

The main menu plans in this book are suitable for those following the no breakfast regime and are mainly for lunches or dinners. However, many of the lunches are also very suitable for breakfast and you can always just pick your favourite to start your day.

They are all tried and tested and I have attempted to give the ingredients for 1 serving where possible. Where this has proved difficult because of the ingredient quantities they will be for 2 or 4 servings.

If I have given ½ a can of beans or other split ingredients the remainder can be stored in the fridge or freezer for other recipes or used for a non fasting day meal. This has not been a problem for me because my husband is also fasting so I cook either 2 portions or 4 portions and freeze the excess. This is very handy when you want a quick lunch or dinner on your fasting days.

However, I do recommend that you cook as big a portion as possible, that way you always have a meal in the freezer or fridge. Let's face it; it will be easier on your fasting days if you are not surrounded by food.

If you really do want single portions, try my other book **the 5:2 Diet Meals for One Cookbook**

Recipes use many different abbreviations. Here are the ones used in this book.

Standard UK & US
tsp = teaspoon
tbsp = tablespoon
oz/s = ounce/ s
lb/s = pound/s
fl. oz. = fluid ounce

Metric
ml = milliliters
ltr = liter/litre
g = grams

Teaspoons and tablespoons are level measure.
1 tsp = 5ml
1tbsp = 15ml

Volume conversions
⅛ tsp = 0.5 ml
¼ tsp = 1 ml
½ tsp = 2 ml
1 tsp = 5 ml
½ tbsp = 7 ml
1 tbsp = 3 tsp = 15 ml
2 tbsp = 1 fl oz = 30 ml
¼ cup = 4 tablespoons or 60 ml
⅓ cup = 90 ml
½ cup = 4 fl oz or 125 ml

⅔ cup = 160 ml
¾ cup = 6 fl oz or 180 ml
1 cup = 16 tbsp or 8 fl oz or 250 ml
1 pint = 2 cups or 500 ml
1 quart = 4 cups or 1 liter

Weight Conversions
½ oz = 15g
1 oz = 30g
2 oz = 60g
3 oz = 85g
¼ pound = 4 oz = 115g
½ pound = 8 oz = 225g
¾ pound = 12 oz = 340g
1 pound = 16 oz = 454g

Oven Temperature Conversions
200 F = 95 C
250 F = 120 C
275 F = 135 C
300 F = 150 C
325 F = 160 C
350 F = 180 C
375 F = 190 C
400 F = 205 C
425 F = 220 C
450 F = 230 C

Ovens vary so cooking times are only approximate. Always preheat your oven and for fan-assisted ovens reduce the temperature by 20°F or see the manufacturer's instructions for your oven.

Portion Sizes

Portion sizes are a general guide but are based on the calories given. Appetites are different but if you want to lose weight you must stick to the portion size.

Oil - Water Spray

Frying, even shallow frying is not recommended as it can add a lot of calories to any meal. I recommend using the 1 calorie oil sprays that are readily available. Alternatively you can make up a solution of 1 part oil to 8 parts water and store it in one of those plastic bottles used as plant de-misters that you can get from any store or garden centre.

When you need to broiler or dry fry, a few sprays of either is enough to lubricate the broiler wire or pan to stop the food sticking. Give the bottle a good shake before using and I recommend sunflower or rapeseed oil. You can even spray the food with this mixture to stop it drying out when you broil or oven frying.

MEAL PLANS

The following meal plans
are for 500 & 600 calories per day
Eating Two Meals Only

Day 1 - 360 kcal

1st Meal - 140 calories

Make a sandwich using the following:

1 Warburton's Thin or other 100 calorie
roll
1 medium tomato cut into 4 slices
4 good slices cucumber
Small squirt low calorie salad cream

Men can have 2 Thins (add 100 calories)
but use the same ingredients sliced thinner.

2nd Meal - 220 calories
Spinach & Mushroom Pie
Good Portion Steamed Broccoli

Spinach & Mushroom Pie - 220 kcal

This is truly one of the most delicious low calorie meals I cook. The wholegrain mustard gives it a lovely flavour and I could eat this every day, even on my non fasting days. It is so filling that I can't believe the calorie count on the quantity of filling.

Serves 2 – 220 calories per serving
***Suitable for freezing
Preparation - 15 minutes
Cooking - 40 minutes

Ingredients

- 200g / 8oz baby spinach or frozen spinach blocks
- 1 cal oil spray
- 250g / 10oz mixed small mushrooms such as chestnut / button / shitake
- 1 garlic clove
- 125ml / 4 fl oz low sodium vegetable stock

- 150g / 6oz cooked new potatoes
- 1 tbsp wholegrain mustard
- 1 tsp grated nutmeg
- 1 heaped tbsp reduced fat crème fraiche
- 2 sheets filo pastry
- 150g / 6oz each of green beans and broccoli

Method

Heat oven to 200° C / 180° C fan / Gas Mark 6

Quarter the mushrooms, crush the garlic, and cut the cooked potatoes into bite size chunks. Wilt spinach in a colander by pouring a kettle of boiling water over it.

Heat 5 pumps of the oil in a large frying pan and cook the mushrooms on a high heat until slightly browned. Add the crushed garlic and cook for another minute.

Add the stock, nutmeg, mustard and potatoes, bring to the boil and simmer for a couple of minutes until reduced slightly. If using frozen spinach blocks add at this stage and cook until spinach has defrosted. Remove from the heat and season with salt and freshly ground black pepper.

Add the crème fraiche and wilted spinach and mix well. Tip into a suitable pie dish or dishes if only having one portion and allow to cool for about 5 minutes.

Lay the filo sheets onto a flat surface and spray with a low cal oil spray or use the oil and water spray. Quarter the sheets and scrunch each piece and lay on top of the pie filling until dish is covered.

If only baking one portion leave off the filo pastry at

this stage and freeze pie filling only in a suitable container which you can defrost for another day.

Bake for 25 minutes until crispy and golden.

*****Filo pastry usually comes in packs of 10 or so. I usually unravel them and fold each sheet into small squares, put greaseproof or foil between each square to separate and freeze in a suitable container. I then just take out what I need. Make sure when you are defrosting that you keep them well wrapped with foil or cling film or they will dry out and fall to pieces.

Day 2 - 395 kcal

Meal 1 - 160 calories

1 portion easy mixed salad - 40 calories
1 portion potato salad - 120 calories

Meal 2 - 235 calories

Pork Chops with Roasted Vegetables

Homemade Potato Salad - 120 kcal

This potato salad can be made in bigger batches and served at lunch or dinner with your other chosen foods. At only 120 calories a serving it makes a nice lunch with chopped tomato and 6 thick slices of cucumber (25 kcal) or Easy Mix Salad (40 kcal)

Makes 1 portion - 120 calories
Preparation - 10 minutes
Cooking - 20 minutes

Ingredients

- 125g / 4½ oz small new potatoes
- 1 tbsp low-fat salad cream
- 1 tbsp low-fat Greek yogurt
- ½ tsp Dijon mustard
- 3 spring onions
- ¼ of a cucumber

Method

Cut the potatoes into roughly 2cm chunks and bring to the boil in a pan of lightly salted water and cook for 10-15 minutes or until soft.

Mix together the low-fat salad cream and yogurt, add the mustard and mix it in well.

Drain the potatoes and put them in a large bowl. When they have cooled a little, stir in the mayonnaise mixture and leave to cool completely.

Chop the spring onions and cucumber and add them to the cold potato salad, mix well, season to taste and serve.

Easy Mixed Salad 40 kcal

You can have this salad for lunch or dinner. It is a staple of my fasting days and I will often eat this for lunch with either a cold veggie sausage or a one egg omelette either hot or cold. I will also eat this salad on my non-fasting days with a bigger omelette because it is easy to make, very good to eat and keeps me off the bread and cakes.

Serves 1 - 40 calories
Preparation 5-10 minutes
Cooking - none

Ingredients

- 1 tomato
- 2 sticks celery
- 6 thick slices of cucumber,
- 2 spring onions
- 1 tbsp of reduced fat salad cream (20cal)
- Squeeze of balsamic glaze

Method

If you prefer you can peel the celery and then chop or slice all salad ingredients. Stir salad cream into the prepared salad. You can use low calorie mayonnaise if preferred but add another 50 calories. I have tried low calorie mayonnaise but because they have taken the oil out to reduce the calories it is quite tasteless and dry. I much prefer salad cream, it has a lot more bite.

Drizzle over a little balsamic glaze for a bit more flavour if liked.

Pork &Roasted Vegetables - 235 kcal

Simple dish to prepare and cook but very filling and enjoyable.

Serves 2 – 235 calories per serving
Preparation – 10 minutes
Cooking – 25-30 minutes

Ingredients

- 1 large carrot
- 1 red pepper
- 1 courgette
- 1 cal oil spray
- 2 good size pork chops
- ¼ tsp paprika
- 50g / 2 oz watercress

Method

Preheat the oven to 200°C / fan 180°C / Gas 6

Peel and slice the carrot and slice the courgette. De-seed and chop the red pepper. Place in a roasting tin and spray with oil, mixing well. Season and roast for 25-30 minutes.

Meantime, heat a grill / griddle pan or broiler. Sprinkle the pork chops with the paprika and cook for 5 minutes each side.

Remove the vegetables from the oven and stir in the watercress. Serve with the pork chop.

Notes

Day 3 - 500 kcal

Meal 1 - 250 calories

Butternut Squash Soup

1 Warburton's Thin or similar 100 kcal roll

Meal 2 - 250 calories

Tuna Steak with Bean Salad

Butternut Squash Soup - 150 kcal

This is a thick and warming soup that can be stored or frozen for another fasting day.

Serves 4 - 150 calories a portion
***Suitable for freezing
Preparation - 10-15 minutes
Cooking - 25-30 minutes

Ingredients

- 1 cal oil spray
- 1 small onion, chopped
- 1 clove of garlic, chopped
- 1 small butternut squash – about 250g / 9oz
- 1 litre / 1¾ pints / 4 cups of vegetable stock
- 1 pinch cayenne pepper

Method

Heat 5 pumps of the oil in a large pan. Add the onion and garlic and cook very gently for about 5 minutes until translucent and sticky but not burnt.

Prepare the squash by cutting into quarters; take out the seeds and then peel. Cut the remaining flesh into small chunks and when onion is ready, add the squash to the pan.

Stir, add the stock and cayenne pepper and bring to a low simmer. Lower the heat and cook for about 20 minutes.

When squash is ready, leave to cool slightly and either use a blender or mash it by hand. Season to taste and add a little more hot stock or water if the soup is too thick.

Tuna Steaks, Salad & Beans - 250 kcal

This recipe is still one of our favourites because you can change the Tuna to almost any other meat or fish. Try is with fishcakes, salmon fillets, steak etc. The variations are endless just watch the calorie count.

Serves 2 - 250 calories per serving
Preparation - 5 minutes
Cooking - 10 minutes

Ingredients

- 2 x 100g / 4 oz Tuna Steaks
- 150g / 5 oz mixed salad leaves or rocket
- 400g / 14 oz Cannellini Beans, drained & rinsed
- 2 or 3 garlic cloves, sliced
- Bunch spring onions, sliced
- 1 cal oil spray
- 2 tbsp lemon juice

Method

Cook Tuna for a few minutes each side until cooked as you like it, or if using frozen cook according to packet instructions.

At the same time, in a small pan, sauté the garlic in 5 pumps of the oil spray for a few seconds taking care not to burn it and then add the drained and rinsed beans and lemon juice.

Cook for a few more minutes and spoon over the arranged salad leaves. Sprinkle over the spring onions, drizzle some balsamic glaze and serve with the Tuna steaks

Notes

Day 4 - 435 kcal

Meal 1 - 105 calories

Canned Tuna Salad

Meal 2 - 330 calories

Pork Stroganoff & Rice

Canned Tuna Salad - 105 kcal

When we first started the 5:2 diet we had this for lunch every fasting day. It is very tasty and filling and we still have it often because it is so simple to do. We sometimes substitute the tuna for a 2 egg omelette which we leave to go cold and chop it up.

Serves 1 - 106 calories
Preparation - 5 minutes

Ingredients

- 1 tomato
- 2 sticks celery
- 5 thick slices of cucumber,
- 1 spring onion
- ½ tin of tuna in spring water drained
- 1 tbsp of low-fat salad cream (20 cals)
- drizzle of balsamic glaze

Method

Chop or slice all salad ingredients to the size and shape you prefer. Mix the salad cream into the Tuna and stir into the prepared salad. (You can keep the other half in the fridge and use for your next fasting day lunch or use it for a sandwich on a non fasting day.)

You can also use low calorie mayonnaise if preferred but you will need to add another 50 calories.

Drizzle over a little balsamic glaze and a few basil leaves if you have them for a bit more flavour.

Pork Stroganoff & Rice - 330 kcal

Use tender pork fillet to make this quick but delicious dish. The mushrooms and green pepper blend well with the tomato and yogurt sauce. If you eat it without the rice the calorie count drops to 195

Serves 2 – 330 calories per serving
***Suitable for freezing
Preparation - 10 minutes
Cooking - 30 minutes

Ingredients

- 175g / 6 oz lean pork fillet
- 1 cal oil spray
- 1 small onion
- 1 garlic clove – crushed
- 15g / ½ oz plain flour

- 1 tbsp tomato puree
- 225g / 7½ fl oz / 1 cup of chicken or vegetable stock
- 75g / 3 oz button mushrooms
- 1 medium green bell pepper
- ½ tsp ground nutmeg
- 2 tbsp low-fat natural yogurt

To serve

- 75g / 3 oz dry weight basmati rice
- 1 tbsp natural yogurt

Method

Chop the onion, slice the mushrooms and de-seed and dice the green pepper. Trim the meat of all fat and skin and cut into 1cm or ½ inch slices.

Heat a large pan, add 10 pumps of the oil and fry the pork, garlic and onion for 5 minutes until meat is slightly browned. Add the flour and tomato paste and stir through, then add the stock, a little at a time and mix well.

Add the mushrooms, pepper, seasoning and nutmeg, bring back to the boil and simmer on a low heat for about 20 minutes.

Meanwhile cook the rice in a pan of boiling water for about 12 minutes or as directed on the packet. Drain and keep warm. Remove the stroganoff from the heat, stir in the yogurt and serve with the rice in warmed bowls.

Notes

Day 5 - 445 kcal

Meal 1 - 150 calories

Hearty Potato & Leek Soup

Meal 2 - 305 calories

Chicken Salad with Red Pepper Couscous

Hearty Potato & Leek Soup - 150 kcal

This soup is so delicious, you really should make bigger batches of it and freeze for convenience.

Serves 1 - 150 calories a portion
***Suitable for freezing
Preparation - 15 minutes
Cooking - 45 minutes

Ingredients

- 250g/8oz small leeks, untrimmed
- 100g / 3½ oz potatoes
- 1 cal oil spray
- 100g / 3½ oz button mushrooms
- A few sprigs of Tarragon, stalks removed
- 80ml / 3 fl oz / ⅓ cup of skimmed milk

Method

Trim the leeks, cut into thin slices and place in cold water to get rid of any soil.

Peel and cut the potatoes into 2cm cubes. Heat 5 pumps of the oil in a large pan over a medium heat.

Thoroughly drain the leeks and add to the pan. Cook gently for about 5 minutes. Add the potatoes and tarragon leaves and enough water to cover. Cook the vegetables for 15-20 minutes with the lid on, then add the milk and the sliced mushrooms and cook for another 20 minutes, adding more water if necessary.

Take out about ¼ of the soup including some potatoes and mash or whiz smooth. Return to the pan, season to taste and serve hot.

Chicken & Red Pepper Couscous - 305 kcal

This is a handy salad dish to make because you can use the ready cooked roasted chicken breasts or leftover chicken.

Serves 2 – 305 calories per serving
Preparation – 10 minutes
Cooking – 10 minutes

Ingredients
- 100g / 4 oz dried couscous
- ½ red bell pepper
- 2 spring onions
- 25g / 1 oz raisins
- 1 red chilli

- 1 small courgette/zucchini
- Juice of ½ lemon
- 1 roasted chicken breast
- 2 handfuls salad leaves

Method

De-seed and cut the pepper into small chunks. Slice the spring onions and the chilli, seeds removed if preferred. Cut the courgette into thin ribbons using a vegetable peeler. Mix the couscous, onions, pepper chunks, chilli and raisins into a large bowl.

Heat up the chicken stock and pour over the couscous mixture. Cover and let stand for 10 minutes.

Fluff up with a fork and then stir lemon juice. Season well and serve with the sliced chicken breast and salad leaves.

Notes

Day 6 - 440 kcal

Meal 1 - 160 calories

Tuna & White Bean Salad

Meal 2 - 280 calories

Chicken Parcels with Mixed Vegetables

Tuna & White Bean Salad - 160 kcal

This makes a tasty substantial lunch or will accompany any meat or fish portion

Serves 2 - 160 calories a portion
Preparation - 10 minutes
Cooking - 5 minutes

Ingredients

- ½ x 400g / 14oz tin of cannellini or other white bean
- 1-2 cloves garlic, chopped
- 1 cal oil spray

- 3 sun-dried tomatoes
- 1 small onion
- 1 x 185g / 7oz tin of tuna in spring water
- 1-2 tbsp balsamic vinegar
- Juice of one lemon

Method

Heat 5 pumps of the oil and sauté the garlic for about 30 seconds. Add the drained and rinsed white beans and about half of the lemon juice and warm over a very gentle heat for about 2-3 minutes.

Meanwhile, blot the sun-dried tomatoes of excess oil using kitchen paper and cut into thin strips. Peel and finely chop the onion and add to a bowl with the tomatoes and the partly drained flaked tuna.

Remove the beans from the heat and add them to the bowl. Mix everything together and then add the balsamic vinegar and the rest of the lemon juice, stir and allow the mixture to cool before serving the salad on a large bed of your favourite lettuce leaves.

Chicken & Mixed Vegetables - 280 kcal

This is a very easy dish to prepare and cook. The chicken breast stays lovely and moist and the vegetables cook just right. As a bonus there will be very little washing up and even if you leave it longer in the oven, the flavours will only increase.

Serves 1 - 280 calories
Preparation - 10 minutes
Cooking - 50-60 minutes

Ingredients

- 1 x Chicken Breast approx 125g / 4½ oz
- ½ medium onion sliced
- 1 small courgette or zucchini sliced
- 100g / 4 oz green beans cut into half
- 1 medium tomato sliced

- 75g / 3 oz broccoli florets
- ½ chicken stock cube

Method

Make a parcel using foil or small roasting bag and place the vegetables in the foil or bag. Lay the chicken breast on top of the vegetables. Make up the stock cube as directed and pour some onto the chicken parcels, not too much, just enough to keep the parcels moist.

Season well with salt and pepper. Add a tsp of your favourite dried herbs or a handful of fresh if you have them. Fold up and seal the parcels, not too tightly or the heat won't penetrate and the vegetables won't cook through. Place in an oven proof dish and cook for a minimum of 50-60 minutes at 190c / 375 F / Gas 5.

Notes

Day 7 - 450 kcal

Meal 1 - 120 calories

Mixed Salad with Avocado

Meal 2 - 330 calories

Vegetable and Potato Bake
Good portion of steamed broccoli

Mixed Salad & Avocado - 120 kcal

A simple salad that goes with anything. Try it on its own for lunch or with a salmon or Tuna steak for your evening meal.

Serves 1 - 120 calories
Preparation - 5 minutes

Ingredients

- 60- 80gm bag mixed salad leaves or rocket
- 3 small tomatoes
- 1 small or half a medium ripe avocado
- Selection of fresh herbs such as basil, mint or chives (optional)
- Olive oil and balsamic vinegar for drizzling

Method

Simply slice or quarter the tomatoes, wash and shred the mixed salad. Mix with the herbs if using and place in a good sized bowl.

Peel and slice the avocado, lay on top of the salad and drizzle with the dressing.

Vegetable & Potato Bake - 330 kcal

This is a substantial vegetable dish with a potato and cheese topping. This is unusual for a low calorie meal so enjoy it. You can also make individual portions for the freezer.

Serves 4 – 330 calories per serving
***Suitable for freezing
Preparation – 10 minutes
Cooking – 25-30 minutes

Ingredients

- 2 medium onions
- 1 garlic clove
- 2 peppers, 1 red and 1 green
- 1 medium aubergine (eggplant)
- 2 medium courgettes (zucchini)

- 2 x 400g /14oz tins chopped tomatoes
- ½ tbsp dried mixed herbs
- 2 tbsp tomato puree
- 900g / 2lb potatoes
- 75g / 2¾ oz grated low fat cheese

Method

Finely chop the onions and garlic. Deseed and halve and slice the peppers. Top and tail the aubergine (eggplant) and cut into small chunks. Trim and thinly slice the courgettes.

Put the onion, garlic, peppers, dried herbs, tomato puree and the 2 tins of chopped tomatoes in a large pan. Bring to the boil, cover and simmer gently for 10 minutes, stirring occasionally. Stir in the aubergine (eggplant) and courgettes and cook uncovered for another 10 minutes, giving it the occasional stir.

Whilst the vegetables are cooking, peel and cut the potatoes into 2.5cm / 1 inch pieces. Boil them for 7-10 minutes until cooked through and then drain. Put the vegetables into oven-proof dishes, depending on your chosen portion size. Place the potatoes on top of the vegetable mixture, dividing equally if using smaller dishes. Sprinkle the cheese on top of the potatoes. **Freeze your other portions at this stage.**

Preheat your grill to medium and grill the dish for 5 minutes until the cheese is bubbling and the potatoes are getting golden and crispy. Serve on warmed plates with nothing else.

Notes

Day 8 - 450 kcal

Meal 1 - 165 calories

Kippers with Easy Mixed Salad

Men can have 2 kippers if liked but add 120 calories

Meal 2 - 285 calories

Brown Rice Mushroom Risotto

Kippers - 125 kcal

Serves 1 = 125 calories a portion
Preparation – 2 minutes
Cooking – 2-3 minutes

There are roughly 125 calories in an average sized smoked kipper fillet, so this will make a quick and satisfying breakfast if that's what you choose. Alternatively, have it with the salad below for a satisfying lunch.

Either cook as normal under the grill/broiler or for a no smell method, place in a suitable dish with a wedge of lemon, add a tbsp milk, cover with cling wrap and microwave for two and a half minutes and voila, tasty breakfast that hasn't used up too much of your allowance.

Easy Mixed Salad - 40 kcal

Serves 1 - 40 calories
Preparation 5-10 minutes

Ingredients

- 1 tomato
- 2 sticks celery
- 6 thick slices of cucumber,
- 2 spring onions
- 1 tbsp of reduced fat salad cream (20cal)
- Squeeze of balsamic glaze

Method

If you like, peel the celery and then chop or slice all salad ingredients. Stir salad cream into the prepared salad.

You can use mayonnaise if preferred but add another 50 calories. I have tried the low calorie mayonnaise but because they have taken oil out to reduce the calories it is quite tasteless and dry. I much prefer salad cream, it has a lot more bite.

Drizzle over a little balsamic glaze for a bit more flavour.

Brown Rice Mushroom Risotto - 285 kcal

This risotto uses brown rice which is a great source
of vitamin B. It is also lower in calories than white rice.

Serves 2 – 284 calories per serving
***Suitable for freezing
Preparation - 20 minutes
Cooking - 50 minutes

Ingredients

- 10g / ½ oz dried porcini mushrooms
- 225g / 8 oz mixed mushrooms
- 1 cal oil spray

- 1 small onion
- 1 garlic clove
- 125g / 4½ oz brown long grain rice
- 450ml / 16 fl oz / 1 pint vegetable stock
- 2 tbsp chopped fresh flat leaf parsley

Method

Put the dried porcini mushrooms in a bowl and pour over 150ml / ½ cup hot water. Soak for about 20 minutes or until the mushrooms have fully hydrated. Drain but reserve the juice and add it to the stock. Roughly chop the mushrooms.

Finely chop the onion and garlic and using a large pan, sauté in 10 pumps of the oil for about 5 minutes on a low heat, stirring to avoid burning. Add the rice to the onion mixture and stir well to coat with the oil. Use more sprays if needed.

Add the stock, bring to a simmer, lower the heat and cook for 20 minutes or until the liquid has almost gone. Make sure you stir frequently to avoid the risotto sticking to the pan.

Cut the remaining mushrooms into quarters or smaller if using a mixture of larger mushrooms. Add to the rice and stir really well to mix in.

Cook for a further 10-15 minutes until all the liquid has been absorbed. Check that the rice has cooked through, adding more hot water or stock if necessary.

Season to taste and add the chopped parsley before serving.

Notes

Day 9 - 380 kcal

Meal 1 - 200 calories

Poached Eggs on Spinach

Meal 2 - 180 calories

Prawns with Cabbage Stir fry

Poached Eggs & Spinach - 200 kcal

Serves 1 – 200 calories
Preparation - 5 minutes
Cooking - 10 minutes

Ingredients
- 1 bag fresh spinach or 200g frozen spinach
- 2 eggs

Method
Poach the eggs as you like them. I find those
silicone poaching pods are great and always deliver a
perfect egg. Rinse the spinach in a colander or sieve and
pour a kettle of boiling water over it to wilt. Drain off
excess water by pressing into the colander or sieve with a
potato masher or other flat tool. Place on warmed plate
and top with poached eggs and season to taste.

You can use frozen spinach if more convenient, just defrost 200g naturally, squeeze excess water out and heat gently until warmed through.

Prawns & Cabbage - 180 kcal

This dish is so quick and easy and I had almost forgotten about it as a very low calorie meal. We used to have this a lot when the cabbage was in season and had a good sized solid heart. Very economical and the prawns lift it out of the ordinary.

Serves 2 – 180 calories per serving
Preparation – 5 minutes
Cooking – 15-20 minutes

Ingredients
- 400g / 14oz sweetheart cabbage or other crunchy cabbage or greens
- 150g cooked jumbo king prawns (defrosted)
- 1 medium onion
- 1 cal oil spray
- splash of balsamic vinegar or soy sauce

Method

Remove the outer leaves of the cabbage and cut in half lengthways. Remove the hard core from the centre of the cabbage and then slice it from the tip to the stalk end, discarding any chunky stalk bits. Wash the cabbage in a bowl of cold water and drain.

Halve and slice the onion and in a wok or large deep sided frying pan heat 10 pumps of the oil and fry the onion for about 3 minutes on a medium heat until starting to soften. Add the cabbage and stir well to bring the onions from the base of the pan.

Add the balsamic or soy sauce, plenty of salt and pepper and then cover the pan and continue to cook for about 5 minutes stirring occasionally.

Check the cabbage is not burning, there should be enough liquid from the cabbage by this time. Carry on cooking on a medium heat, until the cabbage stalks are softened.

When cabbage is cooked to your liking, add the prawns and heat through for a couple of minutes at most. Serve on warmed plates with another dash of balsamic on top.

Notes

Day 10 - 355 kcal

Meal 1 - 175 calories

BLT Sandwich

Meal 2 - 180 calories

Turkey & Vegetable Loaf
Good portion steamed broccoli

BLT Sandwich - 175 kcal

This is a quick but satisfying lunch and you can have because it uses low fat bacon

175 calories per serving
Preparation - 2 minutes
Cooking - 5 minutes

Ingredients

- 1 low calorie flatbread or Warburton's 'Thin' roll

- 1 low fat bacon rasher
- 1 tsp lighter salad cream
- 1 medium tomato
- lettuce

Method

Grill or dry fry the bacon and drain off any liquid or fat. Lightly toast the flatbread and build the sandwich by spreading the salad cream over the flatbread, top with the sliced lettuce and then bacon rasher and finally add the sliced tomato.

Turkey & Vegetable Loaf - 180 kcal

An impressive but easy to make dish, that you can serve as a light supper meal for friends. Cook some baby new potatoes for them and just have some broccoli for you if a fasting day. Alternatively, freeze the other portions for a quick and low calorie lunch.

Serves 6 – 179 calories per serving
***Suitable for freezing
Preparation – 10 minutes
Cooking - 1-1½ hours

Ingredients

- 1 medium onion
- 1 garlic clove
- 900g / 2lb minced turkey
- 1 tbsp chopped fresh flat leaf parsley

- 1 tbsp chopped fresh chives
- 1 tbsp chopped fresh basil
- 1 egg white
- 1 medium courgette/zucchini
- 2 medium tomatoes

Method

Preheat the oven to 190°C / 375°F / Gas 5

Finely chop the onion and crush the garlic. Lightly grease a loaf tin and line it with baking parchment.

Mix the onion, garlic, herbs and turkey together in a large bowl and season with salt and freshly ground pepper. When well mixed, add the egg white to bind it together. You may want to use your hands to get it mixed well.

Divide the mixture in two and press one portion into the tin, firming it into the corners. Thinly slice the courgette and arrange over the meat. Thinly slice the tomatoes and layer on the courgette. Put the remaining turkey on top of this and press down to firm.

Cover with foil and place in a roasting tin. Pour enough boiling water into the tin to come half way up the meatloaf tin sides. Bake in the oven for 1-1¼ hours removing the foil for the final 20 minutes.

Test the meatloaf is cooked by inserting a knife or skewer into the centre of the loaf. The loaf is cooked if the juices are clear and the loaf has shrunk away from the sides of the tin. Serve with a good portion of steamed broccoli and courgettes

NOTES

Day 11 - 365 kcal

Meal 1 - 185 calories

Tomato & Red Pepper Soup
3 x Rice Cakes scratched with low fat spread

Meal 2 - 180 calories

Vegetable Curry

Tomato & Red Pepper Soup - 185 kcal

This makes a great starter or a light lunch and is very easy to make. Make sure you cook plenty for freezing.

Serves 4 - 95 calories per serving
***Suitable for freezing
Preparation - 10 minutes
Cooking - 30 minutes

Ingredients

- 2 red peppers
- 2 garlic cloves
- 1 medium onion
- 1 cal oil spray
- 400g / 14oz tin of chopped tomatoes
- 75g / 3oz potatoes

Method

De-seed and chop the peppers into chunks. Chop or dice the onion and the garlic. Peel and cut the potatoes into good sized chunks and keep in water until needed.

Heat a pan over a medium heat and when warm, add 5 pumps of oil spray, the peppers, onion and garlic and allow them to cook for about 5 minutes until softened. Make sure you stir often so that they don't stick.

Add the tinned tomatoes and potatoes and using the tomato can as a measure use 2 cans full of water to cover.

Simmer the soup for about 20 minutes until the vegetables are done, then allow them to cool slightly and blend until smooth or semi-smooth according to your taste. Reheat and serve.

This makes 4 portions but can be frozen for another fasting day. Defrost or cook from frozen either on stove or microwave.

Vegetable Curry - 180 kcal

You could use a pre-mixed madras curry powder instead of the spices. This could also be made in bigger portions and frozen. You can also use fresh vegetables, just adjust the cooking time to make sure they are cooked before serving the curry.

Serves 1 - 180 calories per serving
***Suitable for freezing
Preparation 5 minutes
Cooking 40 minutes

Ingredients

- 1 cal oil spray
- ½ tsp each of cumin seeds and mustard seeds
- ½ onion
- 1 clove garlic

- ¼ tsp ground coriander, ground cumin and turmeric
- ½ tsp mild chilli powder
- ½ tsp salt
- ½ tin chopped tomatoes
- 2 handfuls of pre-chopped frozen vegetables (choose from carrot, peas, green beans, cauliflower, or anything else you like!)

Method

Finely chop the onion and garlic. Heat 5 pumps of the oil spray and cook the cumin and mustard seeds until the spices start to pop but do not burn them.

Add the chopped onion and garlic, stir and lower the heat to a simmer.

Cook the onions for about 10 minutes until they are translucent and starting to go brown.

Add the remaining spices and the salt, stir thoroughly and then add the chopped tomatoes.

Add your choice of vegetables and then simmer gently for ½ an hour adding a little water if mixture starts to dry out.

Notes

Day 12 - 385 kcal

Meal 1 - 170 calories

Lentil & Spring Green Soup
2 x Crackers for Cheese or Rice Cakes
Scraping of Low Fat Spread

Meal 2 - 215 calories

Leek & Bean Frittata
Green Salad or Steamed Broccoli

Lentil & Spring Greens Soup - 110 kcal

The lentils and greens make a colourful combination and the taste is not bad either. Alternate the choice of greens and spinach for variety.

Serves 2 - 110 calories
Preparation - 10 minutes
Cooking 30-35 minutes

Ingredients

- 100g / 3¼ oz green lentils
- 1 medium onion
- 2 cloves of garlic
- 1 cal oil spray
- 100g / 3¼ oz fresh spring greens or spinach
- 400ml / 13oz / 1¾ cups of vegetable stock or water

Method

Rinse the lentils under running water and cook them in fresh water for 10-15 minutes until just beginning to go soft. Drain and rinse again.

Peel and chop the onion and garlic. Put 5 pumps of the oil in a large pan and cook the onion until soft but not burnt, then add the garlic and lentils.

Wash and chop the greens or spinach and add it to the pan gradually, allowing it to shrink down but keep stirring. When all the greens or spinach are in, reduce it by about half, add enough liquid to cover and cook for about 15 minutes if spring greens, 10 minutes if using spinach.

Allow to cool slightly, blend, reheat and serve.

Leek & Bean Frittata - 215 kcal

An easy dish to make and keeps well in the fridge and is just as delicious cold for a quick lunch for your next fasting day.

Serves 4 – 215 calories per serving
Preparation - 10 minutes
Cooking - 40 minutes

Ingredients

- 250g / 9oz fresh or frozen broad beans (defrosted)
- 2 leeks
- 2 courgettes
- 1 tbsp fresh mint leaves
- 6 eggs
- 75g / 2¾ oz light mozzarella cheese

Method

Slice the leeks and wash out any soil. Thinly slice the courgettes and chop the mint. Drain the mozzarella and cut into very small cubes.

Add the broad beans to a pan of boiling water, bring back to the boil and cook for 4 minutes, add the leeks and courgettes and cook for a further 2 minutes. Drain and run under cold water to cool. Peel the outer skin from the beans and discard.

Heat a large non -stick pan and fry the vegetables with the mint for 3 minutes to remove excess water. Beat the eggs and season with salt and freshly ground black pepper. Pour into the pan and cook gently for 5-6 minutes or until nearly set.

Meanwhile, preheat a grill to medium, sprinkle the frittata with the chopped mozzarella, brown under the grill until top is bubbling.

Slice into 8 portions and serve 2 per person with a green salad or fresh steamed broccoli.

Notes

Day 13 - 410 kcal

Meal 1 - 225 calories

Portion Low Calorie Hummus - 125
3 x Rice Cakes - 90
3 Slices Cucumber - 10
Or
1 toasted or sparsely buttered 100 cal Roll

Meal 2 - 185 calories

Tomato & Courgette Crunch Bake
Steamed Broccoli

Low Calorie Hummus - 125 kcal

Hummus is a great little snacking or lunch food. It is quite filling if you have 3 rice cakes at 30 calories each with a thin slice of cucumber or tomato on top.

Makes 4 portions - 125 calories per portion

Preparation 5-10 minutes
Cooking 5 minutes

Ingredients
- 1 x 400g/14oz tin chickpeas
- 2 cloves of garlic
- juice of 1 lemon
- 2 tbsp tahini

Method

Drain and rinse the chickpeas. Put them in a pan with fresh water and heat gently for about 5 minutes. Drain the chickpeas but keep some of the liquid and set aside.

Crush the garlic, place in a food processor with the chickpeas and lemon juice.

Add the tahini and a tablespoon of the cooking liquid and process until smooth, adding more liquid if necessary.

Tomato & Courgette Crunch - 185 kcal

A tasty and very low calorie dish to use as a main course or as an accompaniment to a main dish.

Serves 4 - 185 calories a portion
Preparation - 10-15 minutes
Cooking - 30 - 35minutes

Ingredients

- 500g courgettes or zucchini
- 1 clove of garlic
- 400g tomatoes
- 2 tbsp green basil pesto
- 4 tbsp fresh breadcrumbs
- 25g mature cheddar

Method

Pre-heat the oven to 220° or Gas 7

Top and tail then thinly slice the courgettes/zucchini. Slice the tomatoes and grate the cheese.

Mix the courgette/zucchini slices and pesto sauce until lightly coated. Arrange the courgette and tomato slices in a single layer in a 2 litre oven proof dish and season well.

In a separate bowl mix together the breadcrumbs, finely chopped garlic and cayenne pepper and cover the vegetables with this mixture. Drizzle with a little olive oil.

Bake for 30 minutes until golden on top and the vegetables are cooked.

Notes

Day 14 - 400 kcal

Meal 1 - 105 calories

Canned Tuna Salad

Meal 2 - 295 calories

Salmon & Ginger Stir fry

Canned Tuna Salad - 105 kcal

When we first started the 5:2 diet we had this for lunch every fasting day. It is very tasty and filling and we still have it often because it is so simple to do. We sometimes substitute the tuna for a 2 egg omelette which we leave to go cold and chop it up.

Serves 1 - 106 calories
Preparation - 5 minutes

Ingredients
- 1 tomato
- 2 sticks celery
- 5 thick slices of cucumber,
- 1 spring onion
- ½ tin of tuna in spring water drained

- 1 tbsp of low-fat salad cream
- drizzle of balsamic glaze

Method

Chop or slice all salad ingredients to the size and shape you prefer.

Mix the salad cream into the Tuna and stir into the prepared salad. (You can keep the other half in the fridge and use for your next fasting day lunch or use it for a sandwich on a non fasting day.) You can also use mayonnaise if preferred but you will need to add another 50 calories.

Drizzle over a little balsamic glaze and a few basil leaves if you have them for a bit more flavour.

Salmon & Ginger Stir Fry - 295 kcal

Serves 2 – 295 calories per portion
Preparation - 10 minutes
Cooking - 10-15 minutes

Ingredients

- 2 x 115g / 4½ oz salmon fillets
- 1 large head of broccoli
- 1 large carrot
- 115g / 4 oz mange tout
- 1 inch piece of fresh root ginger
- 2 tbsp light soy sauce
- 1 cal oil spray
- ½ lemon, sliced

Method

Wash the salmon, check for any stray bones and drain on kitchen paper.

Prepare the vegetables by breaking or slicing the broccoli into small florets. Peel the carrot and cut into dice and slice the mange tout into strips, cutting off the top and bottom first. Peel the fresh ginger and again slice into matchstick size strips.

Put all the vegetables into a large bowl and mix in 1 tbsp soy sauce, put to one side.

Preheat a grill or barbecue and place the salmon on the grill pan, brush with the other half of the soy sauce and grill for 2-3 minutes each side depending on the thickness of the fillet or until cooked through.

In the meantime, heat 10 pumps of the oil spray in a wok or large frying pan and stir fry the vegetables for about 5 minutes on medium heat until cooked through or to taste.

When vegetables are cooked divide between 2 warmed plates and serve the fish on top with a lemon slice and a dash of soy sauce.

Notes

Day 15 - 445 kcal

Meal 1 - 120 calories

Mixed Salad with Avocado

Meal 2 - 325 calories

Low Fat Toad in the Hole
Steamed Broccoli & Carrots

Mixed Salad with Avocado - 120 kcal

A simple salad that goes with anything. Try it on its own for lunch or with a salmon or tuna steak for your evening meal.

Serves 1 - 120 calories
Preparation - 5 minutes

Ingredients

- 60- 80gm bag mixed salad leaves or rocket
- 3 small tomatoes
- 1 small or half a medium ripe avocado
- Selection of fresh herbs such as basil, mint or chives (optional)
- Olive oil and balsamic vinegar for drizzling

Method

Slice or quarter the tomatoes, wash and shred the mixed salad. Mix with the herbs if using and place in a good sized bowl.

Peel and slice the avocado, lay on top of the salad and drizzle with the dressing.

Low Fat Toad in the Hole - 325 kcal

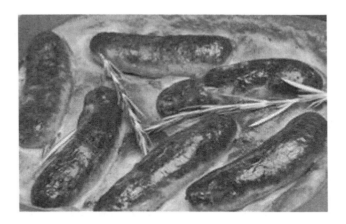

This is a low fat version of toad in the hole. You could use the Quorn or similar sausages if preferred but you should compare the calorie count first.

Serves 2 - 325 calories per serving
Preparation 10 minutes
Cooking – 55-60 minutes

Ingredients

- ½ red onion
- 4 low fat pork sausages or quorn equivalent
- 1 cal oil spray
- 50g / 2oz plain flour
- 1 medium egg
- 150ml / 5 fl oz / scant ¾ cup skimmed milk
- 1 tsp creamed horseradish

- 150g / 5 oz broccoli
- 100g / 4 oz carrots

Method

Pre-heat the oven to 200°C / Gas 6

Cut the onion into wedges and separate the layers. Place in a small shallow non-stick tin or ceramic dish. Arrange the sausages on top of the onions, spray with oil (about 10 pumps) and roast for 20 minutes.

Meanwhile make the batter by beating the egg into the sifted flour and then add the milk a little at a time until all the lumps have gone and the batter is nice and smooth.

Stir in the horseradish and season to taste. When the sausages have been cooking for the 20 minutes, pour the batter into the pan and put back in the oven for another 40 minutes until golden and fluffy.

Serve with the steamed broccoli and carrots.

Notes

Day 16 - 475 kcal

Meal 1 - 150 calories

I Warburton's Thin
Spread of Low Fat Soft Cheese
4 Slices Cucumber

Toast the roll and simply spread with the
cheese and top with cucumber.

Meal 2 - 325 calories

Tuna Steak with Sweet Potato & Carrot Mash
Broccoli & 1 Medium Courgette steamed

Tuna & Mash - 325 kcal

Sweet Potato is actually slightly higher in calories and carbs than white potatoes so you can have either. Personally I prefer the taste of the sweet potato and carrot mash but it's your choice but by using carrot to bulk up the mash you are saving calories. If you do use white potatoes, make sure you only have the same combined weight. This mash also freezes well so you might consider making bigger batches for convenience.

Serves 1 - 325 calories
***Mash is suitable for freezing
Preparation - 10 minutes
Cooking - 20 minutes

Ingredients

- 1 tuna steak approx 125g / 4½ oz each
- 1 sweet potato - 200g / 7 oz peeled weight
- 1 medium carrot
- 1 medium tomato
- 100g / 4 oz of broccoli florets
- 1 garlic clove

Method

Peel and chop sweet potato into largish chunks and the carrots into smaller slices as they take longer to cook. Boil in lightly salted water until soft, about 10-15 minutes depending on size, then mash with a little seasoning but no butter.

Oven bake the tuna sprayed with oil and water mixture for about 20 minutes or if you prefer, griddle for about 10 minutes turning over half way through cooking.

Cut the tomato in half and place in another dish. Peel and slice the garlic and poke the slivers into the flesh of the tomatoes. Drizzle with a tiny amount of olive oil and some freshly ground pepper and bake for about 15 minutes.

Steam or microwave the broccoli as liked and serve with the tuna, mash and baked tomatoes.

Notes

Day 17 - 465 kcal

Meal 1 - 100 calories

Easy Mix Salad
Egg White Omelette

Meal 2 - 365 calories

Butternut Squash Risotto

Egg White Omelette - 60 kcal

Serves 1 - 60 calories per serving

Preparation - 2 minutes
Cooking - 2 minutes

Ingredients

- 3 large eggs or 100g ready egg whites
- a few basil or other fresh herb leaves
- 3 sprays light sunflower oil

Method

Separate the eggs and save the yolks for a non fasting day meal or use the carton of egg whites available in most big stores.

Whisk together the egg whites and a good helping of salt and pepper. Spray the oil into a non stick pan and heat until the pan looks hot.

Pour in the egg whites and cook until ready but not too dry. Serve at once with the herb leaves.

Easy Mixed Salad - 40 kcal

Serves 1 - 40 calories
Preparation 5-10 minutes

Ingredients

- 1 tomato
- 2 sticks celery
- 6 thick slices of cucumber,
- 2 spring onions
- 1 tbsp of reduced fat salad cream (20cal)
- Squeeze of balsamic glaze

Method

If you like, peel the celery and then chop or slice all salad ingredients. Stir salad cream into the prepared salad. You can use mayonnaise if preferred but add another 50 calories. I have tried the low calorie mayonnaise but because they have taken oil out to reduce the calories it is quite tasteless and dry. I much prefer salad cream, it has a lot more bite. Drizzle over a little balsamic glaze for a bit more flavour.

Butternut Squash Risotto - 365 kcal

Risotto is a very easy dish to master once you get the hang of it. This recipe serves 2 but it freezes well so that you can have more ready meals in the freezer.

Serves 2 – 365 calories per serving
***Suitable for freezing
Preparation – 10 minutes
Cooking – 20-25 minutes

Ingredients

- 1 small onion
- 1 cal oil spray
- 1 x 250g / 9 oz butternut squash
- 150g / 5 oz carnnaroli or arborio risotto rice
- 600ml / 1¼ pint / 2½ cups vegetable stock
- 2 tbsp grated parmesan

Method

Chop the onion finely. Peel and dice the butternut squash or pumpkin.

Heat 10 pumps of the oil spray in a large pan and fry the onion until softened. Add the rice and stir until coated in the oil. Add the squash and half the hot stock and stir well. Cook, stirring often until most of the stock has been absorbed. Then add a little stock at a time, again stirring until absorbed.

Repeat this until all the stock has been used and the rice and squash are cooked. The rice should have a little bite but not grainy. Add more stock or hot water if needed.

Add the cheese to the rice and stir well. Cover the pan and leave to sit for 1 minute.

Season well and dish out into warmed bowls. Add a very tiny splash of olive oil to each bowl and serve.

Notes

Day 18 - 455 kcal

Meal 1 - 105 calories

1 Portion Ratatouille

Meal 2 - 350 calories

Vegetarian Sweet Potato Curry

Ratatouille - 105 kcal

This dish can be served with any fish or meat for a substantial evening meal as the ratatouille is only 105 calories per serving. However this also makes a delicious lunch.

Serves 2 – 105 calories per portion for the ratatouille
Preparation - 10-15 minutes
Cooking - 20 minutes plus time to cook chosen meat/fish

Ingredients
- 1 medium onion
- 1 garlic clove
- 1 small green bell pepper
- 1 small yellow bell pepper
- 1 medium courgette

- 100g / 4oz button mushrooms
- 400g / 14oz can chopped tomatoes
- 2 tbsp tomato paste
- 1 tsp of dried mixed herbs

Method

Peel and chop the onion, trim, de-seed and dice both peppers and the courgette. Halve the mushrooms, chop the garlic.

Put all vegetables into a pan and add the chopped tomatoes and tomato paste and stir well. Add the dried herbs, a tsp of sugar and plenty of seasoning. Bring to the boil and simmer uncovered for 20 minutes.

Vege Sweet Curry - 350 kcal

This is a very easy one-pot meal that you will cook again and again just because it is so delicious and quick to do. You will even consider having it on your non fasting days with rice and a naan bread.

Serves 2 - 350 calories per serving
***Suitable for freezing
Preparation - 10 minutes
Cooking - 30 minutes

Ingredients
- 100g / 4 oz red lentils
- 450ml / 15 fl oz / 1¾ cups vegetable stock
- 1 small onion
- 2 medium tomatoes
- 1 tsp turmeric

- 1 tsp garam masala
- 1 red chilli
- 1 large sweet potato
- 2 handfuls baby spinach

Method

Finely chop the onion and chilli. Roughly chop the tomatoes. Peel and cube the sweet potato and shred the baby spinach.

Put the lentils, stock, onion, tomatoes, spices and the red chilli into a pan, bring to a simmer and cook for 10 minutes.

Add the sweet potato and cook for a further 10 minutes or until done.

Stir in the shredded baby spinach and season to taste. When spinach is wilted, serve at once.

Notes

Day 19 - 410 kcal

Meal 1 - 115 calories

Hungarian Vegetables

Meal 2 - 295 calories

Pork Chilli with Beans

Hungarian Vegetables - 115 kcal

This is a very low calorie dish that can be kept in the fridge and eaten for quick lunches on either fasting or non fasting days.

Serves 4 – 115 calories per serving
Preparation - 10 minutes
Cooking - 20 minutes

Ingredients

- 1 onion
- 2 garlic cloves
- 1 red & 1 green peppers
- 3 portabella mushrooms
- 400g / 14 oz tin artichoke hearts in water
- 400g / 14 oz tin chopped tomatoes
- 1 tbsp rose harissa paste
- 1 tbsp paprika

- 1 tbsp tomato paste
- 300ml / 10 fl oz vegetable stock

Method

Roughly chop the onion and crush the garlic. Deseed the peppers and cut into 8 pieces. Quarter the portabello mushrooms, drain and quarter the artichoke hearts.

Spray a large non stick pan and heat until hot. Add the onion and cook for 4 minutes until soft but not burnt. Add the peppers, mushrooms, garlic and artichokes and cook for a further 3 minutes until browned.

Stir in the harissa and tomato pastes and the paprika and cook for a further minute. Add the tin of tomatoes and the vegetable stock, bring to a simmer and cook for 10 minutes until thickened. Serve at once.

Pork Chilli & Beans - 295 kcal

A one pot dish that you will eat over and over again, it's that good. Use tenderloin of pork a really tender cut of pork and good value as there's no waste. Because this serves 4 this is another one for the freezer.

Serves 4 - 294 calories per serving
***Suitable for freezing
Preparation - 10 minutes
Cooking - 30 - 35 minutes

Ingredients

- 1 cal oil spray

- 400g / 14 oz pork tenderloin
- 1 medium onion
- 2 garlic cloves
- good pinch chilli flakes or crushed chilli
- 1 tsp cumin
- 1 red bell pepper
- 1 400g / 14 oz can chopped tomatoes
- 400ml / 14 fl oz / 1½ cups chicken stock
- 250g / 9 oz small salad potatoes
- 100g / 4 oz green beans

Method

Dice the pork into bite sized pieces. Halve and slice the onion and then peel and slice the garlic. De-seed the red pepper and cut into chunks. Wash and halve the salad potatoes. Top and tail the green beans and cut in half.

Heat 15 pumps of the oil spray in a large pan and when hot, season and brown the pork. When browned all over, remove from pan and add the onion and garlic and sauté for a minute.

Add the chilli, cumin and pepper and cook for a further 2 minutes. Put the pork back in the pan with the tomatoes and stock and bring to a simmer.

Add the potatoes and cook for about 10-15 minutes, stirring occasionally until the potatoes and meat are tender.

Add the green beans and cook for a further 5 minutes. Season and serve.

Notes

Day 20 - 415 kcal

Meal 1 - 160 calories

Pea & Spinach Dahl

Meal 2 - 255 calories

Mushroom Omelette with Mixed Salad

Pea & Spinach Dahl - 160 kcal

This dish will warm and fill you up on your fasting day, what more could you want?

Serves 4- 160 calories per serving
***Suitable for freezing
Preparation - 10 minutes
Cooking - 50 minutes

Ingredients

- 1 large onion
- 4 cloves garlic
- 1 thumb size piece fresh ginger
- 1 large red chilli
- 1 cal oil spray
- 225g / 8oz red lentils
- ¼ tsp turmeric powder
- ¼ tsp cayenne pepper
- 1 tsp paprika

- ½ tsp ground cumin
- 1200ml / 2 pints water
- 1 tomato
- juice of 1 lime
- 2 tbsp frozen peas
- 3 cubes frozen spinach

Method

Peel and roughly chop the onion, garlic and ginger. Do the same to the chilli but if you don't want it too hot you can remove all or some of the seeds and membrane.

Heat 5 sprays of the oil in a large heavy based pan and sauté all chopped ingredients for about 5 minutes or until the onion has softened. Add all the ground spices and fry for another couple of minutes stirring well.

Rinse the lentils in a sieve under cold running water for at least a minute and add them to the pan. Stir really well and then add the water and bring back to a boil. Boil at a steady rate for 10 minutes and then turn the heat down to a low simmer.

Continue to simmer at the lowest heat for about 30 to 40 minutes, making sure you stir the Dahl often to stop it sticking on the bottom of the pan. The mixture will thicken as it cooks and when it looks like thick rice pudding, add the spinach, peas, lime juice and the chopped tomato and cook for another 5 minutes and then serve in warmed bowls.

Mushroom Omelette & Salad - 255 kcal

Serves 1 – 255 calories
Preparation - 5-10 minutes
Cooking - 5-7 minutes

Ingredients

- 75g / 3 oz mushrooms
- 2 medium free range eggs
- Handful of fresh Basil or other preferred herb
- 75g / 3 oz mixed leaf or other salad
- 5 cherry or other small tomatoes
- Dribble of olive oil and balsamic vinegar dressing

Method

Slice or chop the mushrooms and cook in a non stick pan until soft but not shrunk too much, remove from pan and set aside.

Wipe out pan and spray with the 1 cal spray oil that you can get from most supermarkets. Lightly beat the eggs together and when pan is hot add the eggs.

Draw the eggs from the side into the middle of the pan until most of the egg liquid has gone from the top of the omelette.

Sprinkle the mushrooms on top evenly, season with salt and freshly ground pepper and when the bottom of the omelette is slightly browned, fold in half, lower heat to minimum and leave to cook very gently for about 2 minutes.

Serve with the mixed salad, tomatoes and dressing.

Notes

Day 21 - 340 kcal

Meal 1 - 90 calories

Vegetable & Citrus Soup
plus
1 Warburton's Thin Roll or Wrap
OR
3 x Rice Cakes
Add 100 calories

Meal 2 - 250 calories

Chicken & Apricot Bake
Steamed Broccoli

Men can have a portion of 100g of new boiled
potatoes -

Vegetable & Citrus Soup - 90 kcal

This tasty soup is a real tummy filler for lunch or an afternoon snack. I suggest you make this in bulk and freeze in individual portions so that you always have a ready prepared meal to hand.

Makes 6 portions – 90 calories per serving
***Suitable for freezing
Preparation - 20 minutes
Cooking - 25 minutes

Ingredients

- 500g / 1lb 2oz carrots
- 2 sticks celery
- 1 yellow bell pepper
- 1 swede
- 2 onions
- 2 garlic cloves
- juice and zest of 1 orange

- 1½ litres / 2¾ pints vegetable stock
- 1 tbsp tomato paste
- bunch chives, chopped

Method

Peel and dice the carrots and swede. Slice the celery and de-seed and slice the pepper. Chop the onions and crush the garlic.

Put the vegetables, garlic and tomato paste and into a large pan, pour over the hot vegetable stock and stir thoroughly. Bring back to a simmer and cook on a low heat for 15- 20 minutes or until vegetables are cooked.

Stir in the orange juice and zest together with the chopped chives and serve in warm bowls for a delicious and filling lunch or afternoon snack.

****Try having a Warburton's thin or similar low calorie bread, either toasted or plain to dip into this soup or 3 rice cakes with a scraping of butter, just add 100 calories.

Chicken & Apricot Bake - 250 kcal

Chicken and apricots go well together and make a nice change from the usual fillings for chicken.

Serves 1 – 252 calories
Preparation – 10 minutes
Cooking – 25 minutes

Ingredients

- 1 skinless boneless chicken breast
- 1 small onion
- 1 garlic clove
- 1 cal oil spray
- 2 dried apricots
- 50g / 2 oz spinach
- 2 tsp cumin

- 2 tsp clear honey

Method

Heat the oven to 200°C / fan 180°C / gas 6

Halve and thinly slice the onion and garlic. Finely chop the apricots and chop the spinach.

Sauté the onion and garlic in a frying pan with 5 pumps of the oil for 5 minutes. Season well and add the apricots, spinach and 1 tsp cumin and cook for a further minute or two.

Make a cut in the chicken across the side to form a pocket and stuff the cooked mixture into the breast. Rub the remaining cumin into the top of the chicken and season.

Pour over the honey, put in a small dish and bake for 20 minutes until cooked.

Serve with a portion of green beans or steamed broccoli.

Notes

Snacks

During the day you may often feel that you want to nibble something between your meals. This is quite normal and is usually because you are bored or have been sitting down for a while or even working for a long time and need a break.

If you can avoid snacking your weight loss will be greater but if you really can't, don't beat yourself up about it, just check how many calories you have spare and choose a little something from the list below.

Also remember that men are allowed an extra 100 calories per day, so when you are calculating they may be able to have jacket potato or extra vegetables with their low calorie meal

SNACKS --

Cheddars biscuit -- 30cal per biscuit
Crackers -- 32cal per biscuit
Rice Cakes -- 30 per cake
Ryvita Crackers -- 27 per cracker
1 small apple, flesh only -- 90

Fruit -- per 100g
apple -- 47
apricots -- 32
blackberries -- 25
cherries -- 48
clementines -- 40
cranberries -- 55
grapes -- 60
kiwi -- 49
melon - cantaloupe -- 19
melon - galia -- 24
melon - honeydew -- 28
melon - watermelon -- 31
nectarines - flesh only -- 40
oranges - flesh only -- 37
peaches -- 33
pears -- 40
pineapple -- 41
plums -- 36
raspberries -- 25
rhubarb -- 7
satsuma flesh only -- 36

strawberries -- 27
tangarine -- 35

Vegetables
carrot sticks raw -- 35
cauliflower raw -- 34
celery raw -- 7
courgette/zucchinis raw -- 18
cucumber -- 10
lettuce -- 16
mushrooms raw -- 13

Peppers stalk & seeds removed
green - raw -- 15
red - raw -- 32
yellow - raw -- 26

Potatoes
potato - baked, flesh only -- 77
potatoes new boiled -- 70

radish -- 12
spinach -- 25
spring onions -- 23
mini corncobs -- 24
tomatoes -- 19
tomatoes - cherry -- 18

About the Author

Best Selling author Liz Armond was born and educated in London, UK. She has been an active student of fitness and nutrition for over 30 years. She has always tried to practice a healthy lifestyle and looks for ways to get fitter and live longer.

After trying the 5.2 diet and having great success she put together her favorite recipes adapted for the 5:2 and published her complete series of cookbooks for every dietary need.

Liz is now an enthusiastic advocate for this proven diet and is a firm believer that following this diet and maintaining a healthy lifestyle will achieve her goal of living a long and happy life.

Other Books by Author

Recipes for the 5:2 Fast Diet
The Fast Diet Cookbook
Vegetarian Recipes for the 5:2 Fast Diet
Vegetarian & Gluten Free for the 5:2 Fast
Diet
Gluten Free for the 5:2 Fast Diet
5:2 Diet Breakfast Recipes
5:2 Diet Meal Plans & Recipes
5:2 Diet Meals for One Cookbook
Vegetarian Meals for One for the Fast Diet

Fasting Your Way to Health
Meditation for Beginners

Disclaimer and/or Legal Notices:

Every effort has been made to accurately represent this book and its potential. Results vary with every individual, and your results may or may not be different from those depicted.

No promises, guarantees or warranties, whether stated or implied, have been made that you will produce any specific result from this book. Your efforts are individual and unique, and may vary from those shown. Your success depends on your efforts, background and motivation.

The material in this publication is provided for educational and informational purposes only and is not intended as medical advice. The information contained in this book should not be used to diagnose or treat any illness, metabolic disorder, disease or health problem.

Always consult your physician or health care provider before beginning any nutrition or exercise program. Use of the programs, advice, and information contained in this book is at the sole choice and risk of the reader

Made in the USA
Middletown, DE
25 June 2018